The Alamo

by Kristin L. Nelson

 Lerner Publications Company • Minneapolis

To everyone who has fought for their freedom or for the freedom of others

Text copyright © 2004 by Kristin L. Nelson

This book is available in two editions:
Library binding by Lerner Publications Company, a division of Lerner Publishing Group
Soft cover by First Avenue Editions, an imprint of Lerner Publishing Group
241 First Avenue North
Minneapolis, MN 55401 U.S.A.

Website address: www.lernerbooks.com

Words in **bold type** are explained in a glossary on page 31.

Library of Congress Cataloging-in-Publication Data

Nelson, Kristin L.
        The Alamo / by Kristin L. Nelson.
            p.   cm. – (Pull ahead books)
        Includes index.
        Summary: Briefly presents the story of the Alamo and its
    significance in Texas history.
        ISBN: 0–8225–3599–8 (lib. bdg. : alk. paper)
        ISBN: 0–8225–3760–5 (pbk. : alk. paper)
        1. Alamo (San Antonio, Tex.)–Siege, 1836–Juvenile
    literature. [1. Alamo (San Antonio, Tex.)–Siege, 1836.
    2. Texas–History–Revolution, 1835–1836.] I. Title.
    II. Series.
    F390.N455 2004
    976.4'03–dc21   2002154874

Manufactured in the United States of America
1 2 3 4 5 6 – JR – 09 08 07 06 05 04

Where is this building?

This building stands proudly in the
state of Texas. It is a **fort** called
the Alamo. Forts have strong walls.

The Alamo is a **symbol.** It stands for the fight for freedom.

In the 1700s, Texas and Mexico belonged
to Spain. Spanish **missionaries** came
to teach Native Americans how to be
Christians. They built the Alamo.

After about 70 years, the missionaries stopped teaching at the Alamo. It became a fort. Soldiers lived there.

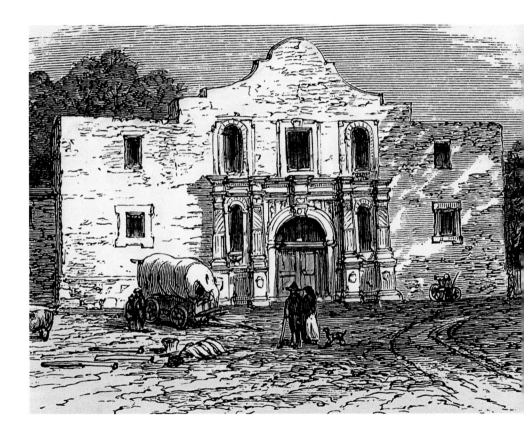

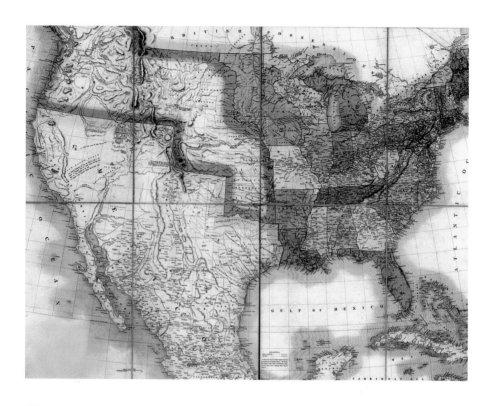

For many years, the people of Mexico
wanted to be free from Spain's rule.
In 1821, they fought a war with Spain.
Mexico won the war.

Texas became part of Mexico. Many
settlers came from the United States
to Texas. They were called Texans.

Texans had to live by Mexican **laws.**
Many Texans didn't agree with these
laws.

Texans didn't want Texas to be part of
Mexico any more. They wanted Texas
to be **independent.** They were ready
to fight so Texas could be free.

General Santa Anna was the **president**
of Mexico. He would do anything to
keep Texas as part of his country.

In 1836, Santa Anna brought his army
into Texas. There were thousands of
men in the Mexican army.

About 100 brave Texans were waiting.
They stood behind the strong walls of
the Alamo.

Davy Crockett was a famous soldier
and hunter. He brought 14 more men
to fight Santa Anna.

Freedom was important to Davy
Crockett. He came to help the Texans
fight for their independence.

For two weeks, the Mexicans surrounded the Alamo. They used their **cannons** to attack the outside of the fort.

The Texans fought bravely. But there
were too many Mexicans.

Finally, the Mexicans climbed up the walls of the Alamo. The final battle began.

The fight lasted for less than an hour.
None of the Texans survived. The
Mexicans won the battle.

People never forgot the men who died
that day. The Alamo became a symbol
of their fight for freedom.

A few weeks after the battle, the United States army fought Santa Anna and the Mexican army.

The Americans shouted, "Remember
the Alamo!" What did they do next?

They captured General Santa Anna.
The Americans won!

Texas became an independent state. Nine years later, it became part of the United States.

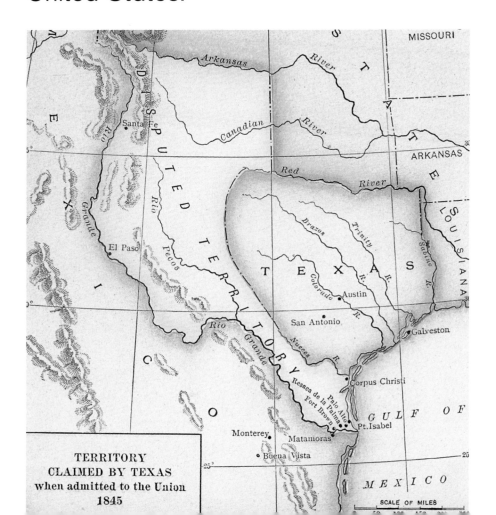

TERRITORY
CLAIMED BY TEXAS
when admitted to the Union
1845

MISSOURI

Arkansas River

Santa Fe

Canadian River

ARKANSAS

Red River

El Paso

Brazos

Trinity

Rio Grande

Pecos

T E X A S

Colorado

Austin

R.

San Antonio

Galveston

Rio Grande

Nueces

R.

Corpus Christi

Resaca de la Palma

Palo Alto

Fort Brown

Pt. Isabel

G U L F   O F

Monterey

Matamoras

Buena Vista

M E X I C O

SCALE OF MILES

DISPUTED TERRITORY

LOUISIANA

Sabine R.

The Alamo still stands. Thousands of
people visit it each year.

The Alamo reminds us of the people who gave their lives so Texas could be free.

Facts about the Alamo

- The name "Alamo" may have come from the Spanish word for cottonwood trees, *alameda.*

- There were only three towns in Texas when it became a territory of Mexico.

- Texas became independent four days before the battle of the Alamo. The men at the Alamo never found out because the news didn't travel fast enough.

- Before the final battle of the Alamo began, Davy Crockett played his fiddle to help liven things up.

- The final battle began at five o'clock in the morning.

- After General Santa Anna was captured in 1836, Texas became an independent country. It was called the Republic of Texas. In 1845, Texas joined the United States. It was the 28th state to join the Union.

- All the Texas missions, except the Alamo, are now parish churches. Masses, weddings, and other activities are held in them.

Davy Crockett

Davy Crockett was one of the men who fought for independence at the Alamo. He had spent most of his life exploring and hunting in America's untamed frontier. The stories he told made him famous. He said that he could hug a bear—and live to tell about it. Davy had also served in United States Congress, where he worked to help poor people own land.

When Davy Crockett heard about the battle at the Alamo, he wanted to be part of it. He thought Texans should live in a free state. He took a few brave men with him and headed for Texas. He lived and died fighting for freedom and for all people's right to independence. He was an American legend.

More about the Alamo

Books

Alphin, Elaine Marie. *Davy Crockett.* Minneapolis: Lerner Publications Company, 2003.

Garland, Sherry. *A Line in the Sand: The Alamo Diary of Lucinda Lawrence, Gonzales, Texas, 1836.* New York: Scholastic, 1998.

Jakes, John. *Susanna of the Alamo: A True Story.* San Diego: Gulliver Books, 1986.

McAuliffe, Emily. *Texas Facts and Symbols.* Mankato, MN: Capstone Press, 1998.

Websites

The Alamo
  <http://www.thealamo.org/>

The Alamo: Five Hours that Changed History
  <http://hotx.com/alamo/>

Alamo de Parras
  <http://www.alamo-de-parras.welkin.org/>

Visiting the Alamo

The Alamo is at 300 Alamo Plaza in downtown San Antonio, Texas. It is open every day of the year except Christmas Eve and Christmas Day.

Glossary

cannons: heavy guns that fire large metal balls

fort: a strong building made to survive attacks

independent: free from the control of other people or another country

laws: rules made by the government

missionaries: people who are sent by a religious group to teach others about that group's religion

president: the leader of a country

settlers: people who make a home in a new place

symbol: an object that stands for an idea, a country, or a person

Index

Photo Acknowledgments

The pictures in this book have been reproduced with the permission of: © Cheryl C. Ricther, p. 3; Independent Picture Service, p. 4; © Bettmann/CORBIS, pp. 5, 17, 23; Library of Congress, pp. 6, 8, 14; © North Wind Picture Archives, pp. 7, 9, 10, 11, 19, 25, 29; The Daughters of the Republic of Texas Library, p. 12; © Stock Montage, pp. 13, 20; Texas State Library and Archives Commission, pp. 15, 22; Friends of the Governor's Mansion, Austin, p. 16; © The Art Archive/Album/Joseph Martin, p. 18; © CORBIS, p. 21; State Preservation Board, p. 24; A. A. M. Van der Heyden Collection/Independent Picture Service, p. 26; © Lowell Georgia/CORBIS, p. 27.

Cover photograph used with the permission of CORBIS Royalty Free.